IN THE FOOTSTEPS

CW00822135

THE CASE OF THE
HOWLING DOG

This book is to be returned on or before
the last date stamped below.

13 MAY 1991

20 MAY 1991

LIBREX —

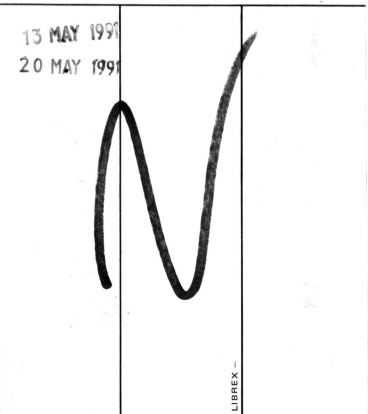

In the footsteps of Sherlock Holmes
The Case of the Baffled Policeman
The Case of the Buchanan Curse
The Case of the Devil's Hoofmarks
The Case of the Frightened Heiress
The Case of the Gentle Conspirators
The Case of the Howling Dog
The Case of the Man who Followed Himself
The Case of the Silent Canary

Published by the Press Syndicate of the University of Cambridge
The Pitt Building, Trumpington Street, Cambridge CB2 1RP
40 West 20th Street, New York, NY 10011, USA
10 Stamford Road, Oakleigh, Melbourne 3166, Australia

© Cambridge University Press 1990

First published 1990

Printed in Great Britain by the Guernsey Press Co. Ltd, Guernsey

British Library cataloguing in publication data
Sharp, Allen
The case of the Howling Dog
I. Title   II. Series
823'.914[F]

ISBN 0 521 38954 2

DS

The cover photograph is reproduced with permission from
City of Westminster: Sherlock Holmes Collection, Marylebone Library
The picture frame was loaned by Tobiass.
p.12 by Celia Hart

The author wishes to acknowledge the indispensable
assistance which has been afforded by frequent reference
to the considerable earlier work of the late
Sir Arthur Conan Doyle.

About the Series

In 1881, Sherlock Holmes, while working in the chemical laboratory of St Bartholomew's hospital in London, met Dr John Watson, an army surgeon recently returned to England. Watson was looking for lodgings. Holmes had just found some which were too large for his needs, and wanted someone to share the rent. So it was that Holmes and Watson moved into 221B Baker Street. It was the beginning of a partnership which was to last more than twenty years and one which would make 221B Baker Street one of the most famous addresses in all of England.

Some credit for that partnership must also go to Mrs Hudson, Sherlock Holmes' landlady and housekeeper. It was she who put up with a lodger who made awful smells with his chemical experiments, who played the violin at any time of the day or night, who kept cigars in the coal scuttle, and who pinned his letters to the wooden mantlepiece with the blade of a knife!

So it is perhaps not unfitting that the only original documents which are known to have survived from those twenty years are now owned by Mrs Susan Stacey, a grandniece of that same Mrs Hudson. They include three of Dr Watson's notebooks or, more accurately, two notebooks and a diary which has been used as a notebook. The rest is an odd assortment, from letters and newspaper clippings to photographs and picture postcards. The whole collection has never been seen as anything more than a curiosity. The notebooks do not contain any complete accounts of cases – only jottings – though some of these were very probably made on the spot in the course of actual investigations. Occasionally, something has been pinned or pasted to a page of a notebook. There are some rough sketches and, perhaps the most interesting, there are many ideas and questions which Watson must have noted down so that he could discuss them with Holmes at some later time.

But now, by using Watson's notebooks, old newspaper reports, police files, and other scraps of information which the documents provide, it has been possible to piece together some of Holmes' cases which have never before been published. In each story, actual pages from the notebooks, or other original documents, have been included. They will be found in places where they add some information, provide some illustration, or pick out what may prove to be important clues.

But it is hoped that they also offer something more. By using your imagination, these pages can give **you** the opportunity to relive the challenge, the excitement and, occasionally, the danger which Watson, who tells the stories, must himself have experienced in working with Sherlock Holmes – the man so often described as "the world's greatest detective".

Chapter One

Death of a Grocer

The events which I am about to relate took place in those early days at 221B Baker Street, when our two most frequent visitors were Tobias Gregson and Godfrey Lestrade. Both were detective sergeants serving in the Criminal Investigation Department of the Metropolitan Police. Sherlock Holmes *had* once described Gregson as "the smartest of the Scotland Yarders", though promptly adding that both Gregson and Lestrade were "the pick of a bad bunch"!

I didn't feel myself qualified to judge either man's professional ability, though my instinctive preference was for Gregson. I suspect it was for no better reason than the man's appearance. His tall, flaxen-haired figure, contrasted sharply with that of Lestrade who was short and dark, with a narrow face which sometimes gave him a quite shifty appearance. The only thing I knew about

Gregson and Lestrade with any certainty was that there was a deal of rivalry between them.

Gregson made no secret of it. Indeed, having interrupted Holmes and myself at breakfast one morning, he gave it as his excuse for calling at such an early hour, being well aware that Sherlock Holmes preferred not to conduct any business before eleven.

"For the last few days," Gregson explained, "Lestrade has been following me round like my own shadow. We're both on the same case, and he wouldn't want me to turn up anything for which he might not get a full share of the credit. But this morning, he's gone to Pentonville to question a prisoner. I saw it as a chance of coming here, without Lestrade demanding to know the reason why."

"Because you wish to consult me about the case upon which you and Lestrade are presently engaged?" Holmes queried. Gregson assumed a hurt expression.

"No, Mr Holmes! I'd not see that as fair. What I've come about isn't anything that either I or Lestrade *can* become involved in. For a start, it would be outside the jurisdiction of the Metropolitan Police. And if Lestrade's right, then it isn't in anybody's jurisdiction, because there's no crime and, according to Lestrade, not even a mystery. So you could say that what's brought me here is nothing more than my own curiosity."

"I confess, Mr Gregson," Holmes remarked,

"that you have already aroused mine. You'll take coffee with us?"

Gregson declined.

"You'll agree, Mr Holmes, that investigating the loss of various items is part of a policeman's stock in trade. And coming, as they do, in all manner of sorts, shapes and sizes not, you might think, likely to give cause for much surprise. Only here's somebody claiming to have lost not just a relative, but the whole of the house that the man once lived in!"

Holmes paused in the act of replenishing his coffee cup. "You did say, 'a house'?"

"A house," Gregson confirmed, "though I'm afraid that the story of its disappearance is one which is somewhat involved. I'll try to omit as much of the detail as would seem to be of no importance."

Holmes resumed the pouring of his coffee. "I should prefer, Mr Gregson, that you omit nothing."

From the length of time it took Gregson to recount his unusual tale, I feel sure he did "omit nothing". I, with the benefit of hindsight, propose greatly to shorten that account, whilst omitting nothing which was to prove significant in the subsequent investigation.

Gregson's story had begun three days previously, with the arrival at Scotland Yard of a Mrs Henry Harper, an American lady. She had insisted upon speaking to a senior detective and had eventually been shown into the office which Gregson shared with Lestrade.

Mrs Harper had been very recently widowed. The story which she had to tell concerned the circumstances surrounding her husband's death but, since that had occurred in Wales, and had already involved the local police, it had become apparent at an early stage of the interview that it was not properly a matter of concern to Scotland Yard.

"You would expect," Gregson said, "that the interview would have been terminated at that point. But then, Mr Holmes, you've not met Mrs Henry Harper! She very simply refused to move until we had listened to the whole of her story – and that story starts more than 70 years ago!"

....

Henry Harper was born in 1811 in a house hard by the Liverpool docks. His father was first mate aboard the *Aphrodite*, a vessel which ran the Atlantic crossing from Liverpool to Charleston in South Carolina, returning with cargoes of American cotton for the spinning mills of Manchester. The *Aphrodite* left Charleston harbour on the morning tide of August 4th, 1819, bound for Liverpool. She was never seen again. Henry Harper was then eight years old. Two years later, Henry's mother died of a fever.

To the boy's knowledge, he was left with only one living relative, his father's elder brother, Thomas. Henry knew little of the man except that like his own father, Thomas had been a sailor – a ship's carpenter in Nelson's navy, who had fought at Trafalgar. It was several years since he had left the sea, and Thomas had come only once to Liverpool, seeking news of his brother. It was at that time when the *Aphrodite* was long overdue and the vessel's owners had told Henry's mother that there was no longer hope. She must presume her husband dead, lost at sea.

Thomas had said that all he could offer his late brother's wife was a few pounds, and his sympathy. But he'd added that if her need were ever truly desperate, then she must come to him. He had drawn a map which showed how she might reach the place where he lived.

After his mother's death, Henry had found the map among her few papers and had recognised it. With no idea of the length or difficulty of the journey, little money, and only what food and clothing he could carry, Henry Harper had set out on foot to find his uncle.

"We will assume," Gregson said, "that the uncle's house was near to a village called Cwmddu. It was in those days no more than a few houses, perhaps hardly even deserving to be called a 'hamlet'."

"You imply some doubt as to the whereabouts of this house," Holmes interrupted.

"And there is," Gregson answered, "but I can see that leading us into a deal of confusion. For the present, I'll say that the uncle *did* live there, and allow you to draw your own conclusions, Mr Holmes."

"You may be sure of my doing that, Mr Gregson. But please continue."

"It's in a part of Wales which they call the Black Mountains. It would help greatly, Mr Holmes, if we had a map. I should have brought one."

A map was found and spread out on the table, the breakfast dishes being placed on the floor in order to accommodate it. Gregson was at some pains to show us the exact location of the house, describing also, the detail of its appearance, its immediate setting and the character of the surrounding countryside.

Since all of that detail will emerge later, I will say only that the house occupied an isolated position in a wood a mile from Cwmddu, itself a small village some three miles south of the market town of Hay, which is in the Welsh county of Brecknockshire. Nothing, it seems, was known of Henry Harper's journey from Liverpool to the Black Mountains. He did find his uncle's house, but was by then, in a state described as "ill, starving and close to complete exhaustion".

It was at about this point in Gregson's story that there emerged a first hint of mystery. The isolation of Thomas Harper's house was not unusual. There are still many like it in that part of the country, though some of them are mere hovels. Nor was it unusual that Harper was almost self-supporting, having a goat and a horse, growing his

Author's addition, drawn from maps of about 1880

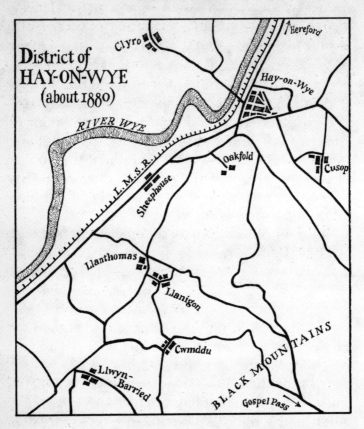

own vegetables, and having an abundance of wild game in the fields and woods around him. The horse was used for the rare journey to Hay to purchase such things as flour and clothing, things which he could not himself produce.

Thomas Harper was also the owner of a large black dog. Doubtless an exaggeration, but the young Henry had described it as as big as the wild ponies he'd seen roaming on the mountains. It was, he said, a creature of most terrifying appearance. Yet the dog, Colossus, named after the ship in which Thomas had fought at Trafalgar, was in truth of the gentlest of natures which in every way belied its fearsome aspect.

But I have not yet touched upon the mystery. Thomas Harper had made it plain that Henry might stay with him for as long as it took him to recover from the effects of his journey, but no longer. He might have given as his reason that it was too lonely a spot for a boy to grow up in. He might have said it was no place to learn the things a boy would need if, one day, he was to venture into the wider world to make a living. But he did not. He gave no reason – not in any words. But Henry had sensed that something was wrong, something which he had not until much later been able to put into words, "It was like the man lived in a state of siege." When Henry was well enough to walk, he was told never to wander far, to avoid any people he might see and, if possible, not to be seen himself – especially so on occasions when accompanied by Colossus who had very soon taken to following him about.

A month passed. Henry, fully recovered in health, must have regarded his new surroundings as near idyllic, but his uncle was not to be moved in his determination that the boy must leave. Henry had talked of America, a place of which his father must often have spoken. He saw it as a land of opportunity and had expressed a wish to go there one day. Thomas Harper now offered him that opportunity – much sooner than the boy could ever have expected and in circumstances where the boy must have felt he had no other real choice. Thomas had given him money and a letter addressed to a firm of London lawyers. He had taken him to Hay, bought him new clothes, and put him on a coach which in two days would bring him to London. A parson called Venables, who was making the same journey, had undertaken to see the boy to his destination.

....

It is my intention to cover the next sixty years of Henry Harper's life in as few words as I am able. It is not because those years were unremarkable – I'm sure that was not so – but because they have little actual bearing upon this case.

Henry never knew the contents of the letter which he delivered to the London lawyers, nor the reasons for the generous assistance which they afforded him. It may be that Thomas Harper had called upon some debt of honour from the time of his service with the navy. It matters only that Henry was found comfortable lodgings with a kindly woman and, within three months, arrangements had been made for him to accompany a respectable Dorset family who were emigrating to America to farm land in South Dakota.

Henry Harper remained with that family for eight years, working for them on their farm. At eighteen, having already shown some natural talent for business, he had accumulated enough money to open his own grocery store. It was to be the first of many. "Harper's Groceries" became a household name in the Dakotas and the neighbouring state of Minnesota. Already a rich man, a number of government contracts acquired during the civil war had made him still richer. At the age of fifty-two, Henry Harper married Catherine McKenzie, a women ten years younger than himself and the daughter of a wealthy banker – the present Mrs Henry Harper. The Harper Empire flourished.

At seventy-one, Henry Harper suffered some severe illness, from which he recovered, but which left him with a serious heart condition. Now condemned to leading the existence of a semi-invalid, and with but few more years of life in prospect, he retained one last ambition – to revisit the place where it had all begun, a house at the foot of the Black Mountains, once the home of his great benefactor, Thomas Harper.

"As you can imagine, Mr Holmes," Gregson

went on, "a journey which involved the crossing of the Atlantic, was seen by both his wife and his medical advisers as probable suicide. His wife must have thought it even more so when, having reached London, he announced his intention of leaving her behind and making the journey to Wales alone. It was, he said, in the nature of being a very personal 'pilgrimage' and thus something which he could not share, not even with his wife.

"He left London on the 25th. His wife heard nothing for ten days, then she was visited by the police. Her husband had been found dead that morning, apparently of natural causes.

"I said that Mrs Harper was a remarkable woman. It will not surprise you when I say that she took the first train out of London, determined to satisfy herself upon the exact circumstances surrounding her husband's death."

Henry Harper had been found dead in the early morning by a passing shepherd. The body was lying on the roadside by a gate in a stone wall which, at that point, separates a rough road from an area of woodland. It was at a spot about a mile from the village of Cwmddu.

"The same spot which you earlier pointed out on the map?" Holmes asked.

"The same," Gregson answered, "and you will shortly see the reason why I suggested that it could cause some confusion."

"I already do see, but do go on."

"The local police had pieced together most of

the story. That did not prevent Mrs Harper from conducting her own investigation, with what appears to have been remarkable thoroughness."

It is not clear how Henry Harper had set about finding such a remote spot in an area of which he had but brief experience, and that sixty years before. Suffice it to say that he did believe that he'd found it, and within a space of only three days. His certainty that it was the exact spot, hung mainly upon two things, the wall and the gate by which he was found dead. In that part of the country, stone walls are uncommon, boundaries being marked by thick, lush hedges. The gate was oak, but the gateposts were of well seasoned yew. Yew outlasts oak, many times, but few are willing to work it, for it will blunt the best axe in a few strokes. Those unusual facts, together with smaller recollections of detail, convinced Henry Harper that he had only to open the gate and walk a short distance into the wood to find the house of Thomas Harper, or at least what remained of it.

He found nothing, either where he remembered the house to be, or anywhere around it. Nor could a house ever have stood there. It was all trees, many of them oak. If their appearance left him in any doubt as to their age, counting the annual rings on the stumps of some which had been felled, suggested that many had stood in that same spot for hundreds of years!

Considerably puzzled, he renewed his search. He found three people still alive, all in their eighties, who were living in Cwmddu when the young Henry Harper was staying with his uncle. Two still lived in Cwmddu and one in Hay. None knew of a house in the place Henry described. They had no recollection of a Thomas Harper, nor of any large black dog. Henry continued his search, but could find no other place which even resembled the spot he had first found.

On the morning of the day he died, Harper was visited by a Dr Price from Hay, the same man who had examined his body after his death. Harper's heart condition was giving him spasms of considerable pain and he had asked for medical attention. He was then staying at the Gospel Inn, a tiny hostelry in Cwmddu. Price had advised him to take to his bed, and remain there. He would visit him the next day and discuss what might best be done. He was in no condition to be walking around, or travelling back to London.

Perhaps certain that his time was now very short, Henry Harper ignored the doctor's advice. That evening, after an early dinner, he was seen to leave the inn. It is assumed that he had walked to the gate in the wall which he had first found. It could well have been his intention to do no more than sit there and read for a while in the warm evening sunshine. He did have with him a book of the collected poems of John Keats. It was still clutched in his hand when the body was found. Gregson now paused, as if he had finished.

"And that is all?" Holmes asked.

"Perhaps not quite," Gregson answered. "Mrs Harper, and even the local police, did make further enquiries in the area, but could find no evidence of a Thomas Harper having ever existed, or of there ever having been a house which could even vaguely fit with Henry Harper's description of it."

"And there's no question of Harper's death being by anything other than natural causes?"

"None, Mr Holmes. I should have told you that Mrs Harper insisted upon a second medical examination of the body before the inquest. It merely confirmed Dr Price's opinion. Harper died of heart failure."

"You said that you came here out of – your word was 'curiosity'. About what, precisely?"

"I knew you'd ask that, Mr Holmes, or tell me that there was no mystery. Lestrade's quite certain there's none. I know there's a simple explanation of the apparent disappearance of both the man and his house." He paused, "This is difficult to put into words."

"Try."

"If you'd heard the story as Mrs Harper told it. There was such a ring of truth about it, which no doubt I've completely lost in the retelling."

"Not at all, Mr Gregson. You told it well, and you have answered my question. Now I must ask you another. Why did Mrs Harper come to Scotland Yard? She had quite obviously talked with the police in Wales."

"She had and, in her own words, 'got little satisfaction there'. She came to the Yard 'to hire a capable detective'! She is American, Mr Holmes. But she'd read Mr Wilkie Collins' books. You may remember that in *The Moonstone* Lady Verinder hires a Sergeant Cuff."

Holmes grinned, broadly.

"And you regret the passing of that practice in the old Detective Branch, Mr Gregson. From what you tell me of the lady, you might have taken some considerable pleasure in recommending Mr Lestrade for the job!"

Gregson clearly enjoyed Holmes' rare flash of humour, but then suddenly looked serious. Holmes had anticipated the reason.

"And Mrs Harper's next question was whether this small island enjoyed the benefits of an organisation similar to Pinkerton's Private Detective Agency. You told her, 'No'. What else did you tell her?"

"Not your name, Mr Holmes, only that we would give her the names of some private agents whom she could contact – and which we haven't yet done. I did say that I came out of curiosity. I admit that part of that curiosity was whether or not you would see it as a case worthy of your personal investigation. The lady is staying at Brown's Hotel."

"Excellent!" Holmes exclaimed. "And I am obliged to you, Mr Gregson. You were right to come. There is most certainly a mystery here!"

Pages from Watson's notebook

I confess that the way Gregson told his story did leave me with the feeling that there was a real mystery here. But now I am beginning to wonder. There are places I visited when I was ten years old that I doubt I could find again. And that's not sixty years ago!

We don't know by what route the young Harper reached his uncle's house. We do know that the child was ill. We don't know how ill, but it could have been sufficiently so to have affected his memory.

He may never have visited the actual village of Cwmddu or even have known of its existence. I have some difficulty in remembering the name — after only a few hours!

We do know that he went to Hay before he left for London (his only visit!) Looking at the maze of

roads — and assuming he was taken
there on his uncle's horse, he would
have had some difficulty in
knowing in which direction they wen
travelling. If he was wrong about
the direction (and the distance?)
he could have been looking in quite
the wrong area. The only reason
for believing it wasn't, was the gate
and the wall. There must be others
something like it in those parts —
and was his memory of it all
that good?

I must say that I'm surprised
at Holmes not seeing all of those
possibilities straight away!

Chapter Two

The Grocer's Widow

When Gregson left, Holmes sat himself down and composed a short note to Mrs Harper, suggesting that she visit him at Baker Street at eleven the next morning. The note was despatched to Brown's Hotel by hand.

Another client arrived at eleven, and one at two that afternoon. Neither came with problems of a particularly difficult or complex nature, but sufficiently so to require the writing of a number of letters, a task which occupied much of Holmes' evening. In consequence, I had little opportunity to discuss with him the case Gregson had brought to us that morning.

In fact that opportunity did not arise until we were seated at breakfast on the following morning. I knew that Holmes had received a reply from Mrs Harper, confirming her eleven o'clock appointment. I'd also had time to form some opinions myself on the basis of what Gregson had told us. I felt that I should discuss them with Holmes, before Mrs Harper's arrival.

Gregson had admitted to there being a "simple explanation" of the apparent disappearance of both Thomas Harper and his house. I had actually thought of two possibilities! Either Henry Harper had searched in completely the wrong area, or he had searched in the right area, but was quite mistaken in his memories of what he was looking for. We did know that the boy was ill on his arrival at his uncle's house. We did not know how ill. He could even have been in a state of delirium.

Holmes favoured the first of my suggestions. The second, he thought unlikely. His own experience of sparsely populated areas, perhaps contrary to expectation, was that everyone made a point of knowing everyone else.

"Unlike Baker Street, Watson, where we don't even know our next door neighbour! If a Thomas Harper had lived in that area, he would most surely have been remembered. And if, as the boy's account suggested, he avoided contact with his neighbours, he would have been even better remembered for that very reason!"

I had also seen some possible lines of enquiry which might serve either to confirm or disprove at least some parts of the story. There were the London lawyers. That firm might still exist. And there was the family who took the boy to America. They might have had children who were still alive. Gregson had been unable to tell us anything other than I have already recorded, but perhaps Mrs Harper could tell us more.

"Perhaps, Watson. I would certainly be interested in knowing the solution to that part of the story – but it is the disappearance of neither Thomas Harper, nor his house that made me feel the case to be worthy of investigation."

"But surely," I said, "the only possible mystery here *is* the disappearance of a man and his house! You told Gregson so, yourself."

"No, Watson. I said that there was most certainly a mystery here. It is you who assumed I was referring to Thomas Harper and his house. Consider, Watson, what we already know of Mrs Harper. She is a woman of strong personality, enterprising, intelligent, thorough. If any confirmation of that were needed, most of those qualities are clearly visible in the content and handwriting of the note in which she accepted my invitation. Surely, the explanations which have occurred to you, to Gregson, and to myself, have also occurred to Mrs Harper. The woman is rich. If it were merely a man and a house she were seeking, then she has the resources to have organised a thorough search of a much wider area. Yet she comes to Scotland Yard. She is clearly dissatisfied, but I ask myself, 'With what?'. Is it really the disappearances, or is it the death of her husband?"

"But there seems no possible doubt that Harper died of natural causes."

"Precisely, Watson. Here is a man with a serious heart condition. He has been advised against travelling to this country. I do not know that part of Wales, but I imagine that his search could have involved him in some quite strenuous walking. On the very day of his death, he has need to consult a doctor because of his supposedly worsening heart condition. Yet Mrs Harper requires a second opinion upon the cause of his death. That, Watson is the greater mystery."

....

Mrs Henry Harper arrived promptly at eleven o'clock and was shown into our rooms. She was a quite tall woman of very upright bearing. Even the manner in which she stepped into the room conveyed a certain air of confidence. More than that, I could not tell. She was dressed entirely in black, appropriate to her recent bereavement, her face also covered by a heavy black veil. I moved forward with the purpose of conducting her to a chair.

No doubt sensing my intention, she promptly lifted her veil. The face beneath it might, at one time, have been attractive. It was still not unpleasant, but its expression was unmistakably stern. It was not the face of a grieving widow.

"Don't fuss, young man!" she admonished.

I may have looked slightly rebuffed. I felt it!

"I'm sorry," she added, in softer tones. "I realise that you were only trying to be polite. I can see you being quite good with tearful young women. I may be neither young nor tearful, but I would not wish you to think that I don't miss Henry. I do. But we did have twenty good years of marriage. Henry got more than the three score years and ten that the 'Good Book' promises – and he died still being the same obstinate man he was when I married him. Now that matter is closed, so we can get to business."

She flopped herself into a chair in a less than ladylike fashion.

"Which one of you is Britain's answer to America's greatest detective, Allan Pinkerton?"

Until now, Holmes had stood silent, with his back to the fireplace.

"It would be difficult for anyone to fill that role," he said.

Mrs Harper looked approving, less so when Holmes continued.

"Mr Pinkerton *is* British. My recollection is that he was born in Glasgow in 1819. My name is Sherlock Holmes. I am the world's only consulting detective."

"Does that mean that you're more expensive than anyone else?"

"No, madam, only better. And may I also introduce my colleague, Dr John Watson."

"The polite one," she said, giving me a peremptory nod of acknowledgment. "Very well, Mr Sherlock Holmes. I have made enquiries about you, and they say you're good. I'll give you a chance to prove it. You're hired. What do you want to know?"

"Everything, Mrs Harper, after which I will decide whether I am prepared to undertake the investigation of your case."

There were some moments of silence, in which Mrs Harper gave Holmes a long, searching look. If I could read anything into her expression, it might have been that she was calculating the number of points so far scored by each side and, having decided that they were equal, was prepared to suspend hostilities! In any event, her next remark was at least a reasonable one.

"You said in your note, Mr Holmes, that you'd heard the story from Mr . . ."

"Gregson."

"Gregson, of your Scotland Yard. Do you really need to hear *all* of it again?"

"Yes, Mrs Harper. Your own knowledge of events up to the time of your visit to Wales is, of necessity, at second hand. The account which I have heard is at third hand. I would not wish to be misled by some inaccuracy in Gregson's retelling of the story."

The explanation was accepted. We heard the whole story, once more, from the beginning. I was struck by the accuracy with which Gregson had remembered every small detail. Holmes' reaction was rather different. He addressed himself to Mrs Harper.

"I know Mr Gregson to have an excellent

memory. His account and your own correspond almost exactly, not merely in the events which are described, but much of it in the precise words used to describe those events. I must assume, therefore, that having given this account twice, on occasions separated by four days, it is you, Mrs Harper who have used those same words. Please do not misunderstand me when I say that the expression which springs to mind in describing such an account is that it has been 'well rehearsed'. I'm not suggesting it's untrue, merely hoping that you can account for the impression which it gives."

"Very easily, Mr Holmes. It has been, as you say, 'well rehearsed', though not by me. If I heard Henry tell that story once, I heard him tell it fifty times – and always the same. The only bit missing's the picture."

This was something which had not been mentioned before.

"Oh!" Mrs Harper continued, "I doubt whether it's of much interest now. It was a painting – a water colour – and I'd say not a very good one. Henry bought it somewhere before I even knew him. It didn't say who painted it, or exactly where it was supposed to be of. It was one of a series of pictures by a Welsh artist. But Henry said he bought it because it reminded him of his uncle Thomas's place. It was no more than a man with a dog, standing by an open gate in a stone wall, and some trees behind. Henry said it might have been painted in the exact spot, except he said the gate was wrong. I don't rightly recall that he ever said what was wrong with it."

"You wouldn't have it with you?" Holmes asked.

'No, it's back home, hung on the wall. It's one thing of Henry's I'll likely not be keeping. I've had to stare at it for twenty years, and always hated the thing. The dog's got a squint, and if you'd had to sit with a dog squinting at you for twenty years, *you'd* be glad to be rid of it!"

Holmes was gazing at the ceiling.

"Mrs Harper," he said, without averting his gaze, "your husband obviously had a very close emotional attachment to his uncle, the dog, the place – certainly to memories of them, which were clearly in the forefront of his mind, literally till the end of his life. Yet you have said nothing of his having made, or attempted to make, any contact with his uncle, not from the moment he left the town of Hay on his way to London."

There was a very distinct pause before Mrs Harper answered. Yet she seemed in no doubt about her answer when it came – a quite positive "No."

"Henry was just not one for writing letters," she said, "though he probably thought about it."

"And what of the London lawyers and the family with whom he lived for eight years?"

"He never wrote to them neither."

"But perhaps they are still traceable."

"No, Mr Holmes. The lawyers went out of business thirty years ago. There were two partners. They're both dead. I found that out while I've been in London. As to the family, I did try to trace them, a lot of years back, but that was after the war. You can't know what the war was like, Mr Holmes. Whole families just wiped out and nobody knowing what happened to them."

"Yes, I do see," Holmes answered, removing his gaze from the ceiling. "You've told us about your visit to Wales, and I see that my colleague, Dr Watson, has been making notes. It may still be necessary to check that we have full details of the visit, particularly of whom you saw and where they might be found. Other than that, Mrs Harper, I have only two further questions. The police must now have returned to you all the personal possessions which your husband had with him at the time of his death. Was there anything amongst them which could conceivably be of some importance – notes which he might have made?"

Mrs Harper opened the rather large bag which she carried and which had, since she seated herself in the chair, reposed on her lap. She withdrew a quite small cardboard box.

"Apart from his clothes and about fifty pounds in money, everything is in there."

Holmes stood up, took the box, and tipped its contents carefully onto the table beside where I was sitting. There was not a great deal in it – a watch and chain, a cigar case and cutter, matches, spectacles, a leather case for holding sovereigns and half sovereigns (but empty), and a medicinal dropping bottle. There was still liquid in the bottle. I guessed it to be tincture of digitalis. There was neither a diary nor a notebook, not even a pencil. There *were* two or three pieces of paper, bills for lodgings, and what I recognised as a sheet of notepaper from Brown's Hotel. On it were the words, "My wife is staying here." Holmes picked it up.

"The handwriting is yours, Mrs Harper."

"It is, I gave it to Henry before he left London. I don't have to tell you about the state of his health, and Henry wouldn't have thought of carrying it."

"What about the book," Holmes asked, "the one he had in his hand when he was found?"

"I left it at the inn where he was staying. I'm sure it wasn't his. I know he didn't have it when he left London."

"A last question, Mrs Harper. Why did you ask for a second examination of your husband's body?"

"I know Henry didn't have long to live, but I wouldn't like to think that someone robbed him even of one day for the sake of a few dollars – I guess I should say 'pounds'."

"What makes you think that anyone might have?"

"I said he had about fifty pounds, of which four pounds in gold was found on his body. The rest was at the inn. Fifty pounds may sound a lot of money, but Henry often carried a deal more than that. He always paid in cash for everything."

"And you thought that the shepherd who found the body, or someone else . . ."

"You must agree, Mr Holmes, that for people like that it would be a great temptation, specially if they knew that everyone was expecting the man to drop down dead at any minute. A blow on the head even a good shock would have been enough to send him on his way, and with nobody surprised to find him dead."

"But no medical evidence of this."

"None."

"And if I undertake to investigate this case, exactly what is it, Mrs Harper, that you expect me to find?"

"I don't know, Mr Holmes. I do know there's something that's not right about the whole business. Finding out 'what', is what I'd be paying you for."

Chapter Three

A Town of Magic Wells

Our journey to Hay was a tedious one, occupying several hours and requiring three changes of train. Holmes was silent for most of the journey, though that was something which I had expected!

After Mrs Harper left us on the previous day, I had expressed some surprise that Holmes had, after all, accepted the case. I knew that Mrs Harper's treatment of him, almost as the "hired hand", was in itself quite sufficient reason for him to refuse her. The fact that she was clearly rich and could therefore afford to pay a large fee for his services, was not a matter to which Holmes was likely even to have given consideration. And there was another reason for my surprise.

Mrs Harper had added very little to what we already knew about the apparent disappearance of both Thomas Harper and his house. She had, however, given what I would have thought a perfectly good explanation for her insisting upon a second examination of her husband's body.

"You did say, Holmes," I reminded him, "that Mrs Harper would seem to have doubts about the cause of her husband's death, and you saw that as the 'greater mystery'. Surely she's now dispelled *that* mystery."

"No, Watson. She gave a reason – which I do not believe. But let us, for a moment suppose it to be true. It does provide an explanation for her asking for a second medical opinion. But that opinion merely suggested that her alleged fears, that her husband was in fact murdered for his money, are untrue. Yet her doubts, whatever in truth they were, still remain. She said that 'there's something not right about the whole business'. She might have said, 'People and houses don't just disappear', or words of that kind. Yet she said nothing in any way specific. I'm still certain that there's something she has not told us. I'm almost equally certain that, unwittingly, she has! If you are hiding something, Watson, then in speaking of anything which touches upon it, your words are cautious. It may appear as a hesitancy, or an unnatural turn of phrase. I sensed it more than once this morning – little things which I cannot yet put together."

It was a signal that Holmes would probably be silent for the rest of the day. He was! Since I shared Holmes' unfamiliarity with the part of the country to which we were obviously going, I consulted his considerable library. Finding nothing, and it being a fine afternoon, I took a walk around some of London's bookshops. I eventually found two likely looking volumes which I purchased from a shop in the Charing Cross Road. One, I read that evening.

At breakfast on the following morning, Holmes was looking a little red-eyed and confined his conversation to essentials, such as the fact that I had rather less than an hour to pack whatever I might need for what could be a "protracted visit" to Wales. Our train, he informed me, was at 10.35 a.m. Holmes' appearance, together with his economy of words, told me two things. He'd been awake for most of the night, and he'd not yet put together those "little things" of which he'd spoken. It was for that reason I had expected a silent journey.

It did give me the opportunity to read the second book that I'd purchased. I will say of it that though providing nothing I could see of likely value to the purpose of our visit, it afforded me some entertaining reading. It was devoted largely to matters of myth and legend. It was by no means a slim volume, but I had finished it before our train left Hereford railway station for the final stage of our journey to Hay.

Doubtless because of my very recent reading and an impressive view of the Black Mountains, now dominating the whole of the skyline to the south west, I found myself contemplating what manner of country it was that we were about to visit. Hay itself was said to contain five magical wells. Yet even that seemed unremarkable in a land whose traditions were of dragons and druids and whose history was filled with treachery, foul murder and bloody border wars! As passing clouds cast dark, moving shapes on the faces of the mountains, it needed but a little stretching of the imagination to believe that this was a place still haunted by shades of its strange and fearful past.

In truth, I found Hay to be a disappointingly ordinary place. Its centre was dominated by a much dilapidated building that looked something like a house, yet also like a castle, but in other respects Hay looked much like many another small market town. The grey stones of the buildings were pleasantly tinged with pink, but if there was any real surprise, it was that everyone seemed to speak English and not Welsh as I had expected. The next day, we found, was market day and, considering the influx of visitors which that had brought, we were perhaps fortunate in obtaining rooms at the Black Lion, a pleasant coaching inn of some obvious antiquity.

....

If Holmes had made any progress in his thinking, he had not said so. If he had not, then he could well have decided to put that problem aside while he dealt with some more pressing matters. After dinner at the inn he suggested that we visit Dr Price that same evening. Price was the man whom

Harper had consulted and who had carried out the first examination of the body. Holmes had already established that Price lived quite close to the inn, by the clocktower in Lion Street itself.

Hywel Price was a man in his fifties, grey haired, stocky, dressed in rough tweeds – I suppose many people's picture of the typical country doctor. He did not seem surprised by our visit.

"You've met Mrs Harper," he said. "She's a very persistent woman. She was obviously still not satisfied when she left here. I didn't believe then that I'd seen an end to the business, though I wonder what more I can tell you than I suspect you already know."

"Perhaps nothing that is significant," Holmes answered. "But I had thought, since my colleague here is a doctor like yourself, that you might give him a more technical account than would have been appropriate for Mrs Harper, or even myself."

"Very well, Mr Holmes. Perhaps if I address myself to Dr Watson, then you can feel free to interrupt."

Price first described the exact nature of Harper's heart condition as revealed by the post mortem.

"When I first saw him," he continued, "I knew there was very little that I could do for him. He was taking tincture of digitalis for the dropsy – 180 minims a day – more than I'd consider a safe dosage, yet his pulse rate was still high. I decided temporarily to take him off the digitalis and try strophantin. And don't look surprised, Doctor!

You may hear that we still treat pneumonia with fresh sheep's lungs placed on the feet, but it's untrue! At the same time, strophantin is a substance of which I've had little direct experience. It was for just that reason I drove back to Cwmddu that same evening to see how Harper was responding to it. But Harper wasn't there. He'd been seen leaving the Gospel Inn at about eight, but since no-one knew his whereabouts, I could do nothing but return home."

"And the next time you saw him was when you were called in by the police to examine the body?"

"Yes, Mr Holmes. Again, as you'll know, the body was found at six the next morning by Evan Lewis, a shepherd on his way up to the mountain. The police were told. I was called out at, I suppose, half past seven."

Price had begun his account of the position and state of the body, when Holmes interrupted him.

"What I'm about to quote is typical of uninformed gossip, and therefore most probably untrue. It is a reference to Harper's death which I chanced to hear this evening in the bar-room of the Black Lion. It is that anyone who'd seen Harper's face could tell that the man had died of fright."

"Untrue, Mr Holmes, but interestingly enough not without some foundation in fact. Harper's death *was* unusual. I've only once before seen a body in that condition. Rigor mortis had been instantaneous upon death, an instant stiffening of the muscles. It occurs if death takes place when the victim is under great stress. Such stress can be caused by fear. It can also be caused by pain, as I'm sure it was in Harper's case. The face muscles *were* slightly distorted."

My mind immediately turned to our conversation with Mrs Harper. It seemed the appropriate moment to tell Price that she claimed to entertain the idea that her husband had been murdered for his money. I said she had actually suggested that he might have died from a blow to the head or, in her own words, "a good shock".

"I was aware of Mrs Harper's theories," Price answered. "It was my main reason for being less than surprised by your visit. I'll say this. It's not *totally* impossible that Harper died of fright, in the sense Mrs Harper would use the word. But both I and Mr Pearson, the surgeon from St Mary's in Birmingham who carried out a full post mortem examination, share the opinion that it was not the case. And if it was fright, then you must ask what could have frightened the man enough to kill him! As to a blow to the head, there was no unusual bruising anywhere on the body. I know that bruising and lividity can be confusing, but not when examined as skin sections under a microscope. No. He was not struck on the head, or anywhere else."

"Two questions," I said. "I know you estimated the time of death as between half past eight and half past ten on the evening he left the inn. Yet you didn't see the body until the next morning? We both know that air temperature, clothing, the build of the victim . . ."

"Don't go on, Dr Watson," Price replied. "Very simply, I used other means! Half past eight is the earliest Harper could have reached the gate from the inn. By half past ten there was a mist coming down the mountain. The ground under the body was dry."

That answer sounded so obvious, I hesitated to ask my second question – how Price knew that rigor mortis had occurred instantly upon death.

"Partially the facial distortion, but mainly the book, Dr Watson. Harper had a book in his hand. The book was tightly gripped. As you will realise, if rigor had not set in immediately, the book would most probably have been dropped or, if still in the hand, would have been held only loosely."

I had forgotten the book. Holmes had not!

"The book, Dr Price, appears to offer some small mystery in itself – as to how it came to be in Harper's possession. Mrs Harper was sufficiently convinced that it was not her husband's property, that she left it at the inn."

"I wasn't aware of that, Mr Holmes, but I'm grateful that you've told me. *I* gave Harper the book. When I first visited him and told him to re-main in bed, he complained of having nothing to read. I happened to have the book in my carriage and lent it to him. I'd forgotten all about it until this moment. I have to go to Cwmddu in the morning and I shall retrieve it."

Our conversation continued until late into the evening. Having told us all he could of a medical nature, Price did turn the conversation to the other aspects of the "mystery". He wasn't surprised by what Holmes had overheard in the Black Lion.

"The story was bound to become widely known," he said. "First with Harper's own enquiries, then his death, Mrs Harper's visit, the police interest and, of course, the inquest, held in the bar-room of the inn where you're staying, and very well attended! But I think you'll find it generally accepted, at least among the more intelligent, that there is no real mystery. Harper died a natural death, and as to his uncle and the house, clearly the man's recollection of the distance and direction from Hay were simply faulty. It had been sixty years. And even if the wall and gate are unusual, I'm sure they're not unique. I'm not sure about the wall, but I am certain I've seen an oak gate with yew gateposts somewhere in the vicinity of Clyro. I'd still have to admit that it makes a good story, especially for bar-rooms, eh, Mr Holmes!"

Before we left, Holmes took the opportunity to ask the precise whereabouts in Hay of William Price, one of the three people who had lived in Cwmddu at the time of the ten year old Henry Harper's visit to his uncle. The man's house was but a stone's throw away, across the street, Price told us.

"But I would see little profit in your visiting it. William Price is eighty years old, and I'm afraid becoming very senile. He has his rare, lucid moments, but even then, his recollections are unreliable."

"Any relation?" I asked.

"Somewhere in the mists of time, perhaps, Doctor. Price is a name like Jones. There are a great many of us about!"

....

It had been a tiring day and on our return to the inn I went straight to my room. I spent less time than I might in writing up my day's notes. I was anxious only to get to my bed, where I must have fallen asleep almost at once. I was awakened in what I imagined were the small hours of the morning by the howling of a dog. It seemed to be coming from just below my window, which over-looked the inn yard. I was surprised, on consulting my watch, to find it was but half an hour past midnight. I became slowly aware of other noises in the inn and taking it that everyone was not yet abed, hoped that something might be done about the dog, whose howling was not only loud, but of a particularly mournful character. My hope was fulfilled. I heard a door open in the yard, a few words were spoken, and then the door was closed. The howling had stopped. I spent the rest of the night in unbroken sleep.

I found myself most impressed by
the extent of Price's medical knowledge
– I suppose I was thinking "for a
country doctor"! But his use of
strophantin certainly did surprise me.
Even some of my London colleagues
would hesitate to prescribe it.

And the man was right about
instant rigor – a fact which I would
not have known myself but for the
chief medical officer of my old
regiment in India. He'd seen a
few suicides in his time. He always
said that if a man who appeared
to have shot himself had the gun
gripped tightly in his hand, then
you could be sure it was suicide
and not murder. Whatever
writers of fiction would have you
believe it simply isn't possible
to shoot a man, then place the
gun in his hand with any hope
of imitating the death grip of

a genuine suicide.

I suppose that this evening's conversation with Price will have left Holmes feeling disappointed. Price's answers did seem to clear up the last remnants of any mystery. I'm not at all certain that there's anything to keep us here any longer — though I've no doubt that Holmes will decide that tomorrow.

I wonder whether he did work out what it was that he said mrs Harper wasn't telling us!

Chapter Four

Not All Gospel

Holmes and I were not late for breakfast, arriving downstairs within moments of each other, but we did appear to be the last. It must have rained in the night, but the morning was fine, a warm sun rapidly drying up what remained of pools of water still visible on the road outside. I had no doubt that the other guests, there for the purpose of doing some business at the market, had been anxious to make an early start.

We were served at the breakfast table by the landlord himself. He asked if either of us had been disturbed in the night by the dog. Holmes had heard nothing, having a room on the front of the inn. The landlord apologised to me.

"She's no more than a Welsh collie," he said, "but she has got a howl like a soul in Hell's torment. And it was all for no better reason than she'd been accidentally locked out in the yard, and it started to rain. I've never known a dog hate rain like that one, and as you heard, sir, not slow in letting you know it."

He went on to ask if we'd be staying for another night and needing our rooms. Holmes explained that we wished to spend some time exploring the area around the village of Cwmddu and asked how that might best be done. Could we, for instance, hire a trap in Hay?

We were told that we could, but that if we were serious about "exploring" the area, then anything with wheels could prove of more hindrance than help.

"It's the roads, you see, gentlemen. Not bad they are, in the valley bottom. Not so good as soon as you're starting up the mountains. How long were you thinking of doing this 'exploring'?"

Holmes was uncertain. Perhaps two or three days. Then the landlord's advice was that we go first to Cwmddu and take rooms at the Gospel Inn. That would bring us three miles nearer than Hay to the place we wanted to be. The exploring could then be done on foot or, if we wished to venture further afield, he'd no doubt that we could hire a couple of horses.

I asked if the Gospel Inn was comfortable. I was told it was – small with no more than two or three rooms for guests, though with little call on them. The food was plain but good, and the place was quiet.

"No howling dogs!" I joked.

The landlord gave me an odd look – as if I might have given him some offence, but quickly turned the subject to what we might like for breakfast.

....

Holmes half surprised me by suggesting that we spend a little time after breakfast walking around the Hay market. It was unlike Holmes to be interested in anything other than the pursuit of the case in hand. Thankfully, he had not returned to his silences of the past two days, but he was far from being talkative. I wondered if he was not beginning to feel some sense of disappointment. Our conversation with Hywel Price on the previous evening had, at least for me, dispelled the idea that there was any mystery here. It would still have been very rewarding could we have succeeded in finding the actual whereabouts of Thomas Harper's house, but that might prove a daunting task, requiring perhaps little skill but much time and diligence. All I could see that was left for Holmes to do was to question the two people still living in Cwmddu who had been there at the time of Henry Harper's first visit. I did not see his getting any different answers to those already given. And I really could see no point in any "exploration" – other than perhaps to visit the gateway where Harper had been found dead.

Whatever the truth of those speculations, the decision to visit the market proved to be a most fortunate one. As the result of an argument with a stallholder as to the genuineness of what he claimed to be a West African blowpipe and darts, we fell into conversation with a bystander, a parson who eventually introduced himself as the Reverend Matthew Ferris, vicar of the church of St Peter and St Paul in the village of Cwmddu! On hearing that it was our intention to visit the place ourselves, he offered to take us there in his trap, since he was himself returning later that morning.

Mr Ferris's trap was a vehicle clearly designed for two, and for a deal less luggage than Holmes and I had between us! And if the roads in the valley bottom were regarded as "not bad", I could see why the landlord of the Black Lion had advised against attempting the use of a wheeled vehicle on those which were apparently regarded as worse! Such was the discomfort, not to say hazard of the journey, Mr Ferris insisted upon our joining him at the parsonage for lunch, "in some small recompense for my well-intentioned but clearly ill-considered offer of assistance!"

We dropped our luggage at the Gospel Inn, and had but a short walk from there to the parsonage. Cwmddu was a village of no more than two dozen houses, the inn and the church being obviously of the most recent construction, though the place looked too small to justify either. It was a subject which I raised over a most excellent lunch of gammon and spinach.

"There lies a tale," Mr Ferris told us. "We have long needed a church in Cwmddu. The place looks small, but if you include the outlying farms and other dwellings, there is a congregation of never less than a hundred souls. In the past, people had to walk to Llanigon. The need was certainly there, but not the money!

"And then – it must be near twenty years ago – before my time here, the bishop received an offer from a Cardiff businessman. It was to provide a substantial part of the cost of a church, but upon one condition. It was to be named 'St Peter and St Paul'. It was not a condition likely to be refused. I'm sure you've heard of the Gospel Pass, and the legend that it was the way used by Peter and Paul to cross the Black Mountains, they having come to Wales at the request of Caractacus to preach to the Silurian tribesmen."

The building of the church was begun with no reason to suppose that it had been made possible by anything other than a simple act of Christian charity. And that belief was not shaken until another building was begun in Cwmddu – what was to become the Gospel Inn.

Mr Ferris admitted to being uncertain of all the details, but the general intent was very clear. The rapid expansion of the railways and the great ease of travel which that offered had brought many visitors to parts of the country hitherto near inaccessible. Cwmddu's church was no act of charity, but just one small part of an ambitious commercial enterprise! The exact route of the Gospel Pass over the top of the Black Mountains is a matter of no dispute. But, as it descends into the Wye valley, it branches into many tracks, one of which passes through Cwmddu. It might have been the end of the original route – as might many others. The existence of the church of St Peter and St Paul, together with an inn called the Gospel Inn, was intended to remove any doubts, at least in the minds of visitors.

"I suppose it sounds quite humorous now," Mr Ferris continued, "but I am reliably informed that it was intended to build a branch line from Hay to The Gospel Pass Railway Station, and that a number of artifacts were to be added along the Pass itself. I recall St Peter's Spring and The Well of Caractacus!"

"But, clearly," I said, "none of this occurred."

"No, Dr Watson. And some would suggest it was an example of divine intervention. The building of the church *was* completed, but before the inn could be finished, the company promoting the scheme went into bankruptcy, which is also why the inn has only three rooms and not the original twenty for which it was designed."

"A most remarkable story," was Holmes' comment, "and one which makes the purpose of our visit here seem almost mundane!"

"Really, Mr Holmes. Now you do intrigue me!"

Holmes had just successfully used one of his favourite devices. He wanted to ask some questions. He did not want to give the impression that obtaining the answers to those questions was the sole reason for his accepting the vicar's hospitality, which it probably was! He had just put his host into the position of almost begging to hear something that Holmes had intended telling, probably from the very outset of our meeting in the Hay market. I had begun even to wonder if that meeting was quite as fortuitous as it had appeared!

I was not certain that I entirely approved of the manner in which Holmes ruthlessly manipulated people to his own ends, particularly a man of the cloth. Perhaps for that reason, I felt some sense of satisfaction when Mr Ferris, who had obviously heard some of the story before, expressed much the same opinion we had heard from Dr Price. There *was* no mystery.

"It does begin to have that appearance," Holmes admitted, "though you appreciate, Mr Ferris, that having accepted this commission, I feel obliged to explore every last possibility. Perhaps you can even be of some assistance."

Holmes asked Ferris the exact whereabouts of the two women in Cwmddu who were there at the time of Henry Harper's first visit. He asked also about Evan Lewis, the man who had found the body.

"I fear, Mr Holmes, that you may be out of fortune," was the reply. "Mrs Williams suffers from what might be called a deafness of convenience. Mrs Parry achieves much the same ends with her pretended difficulty with the English language. I do speak Welsh, and could of course

come with you to see Mrs Parry but, in truth Mr
Holmes, I don't believe that either of them knows
more than they've already told."

"What of Evan Lewis?"

"A different problem. He's a shepherd. In
summer the sheep are taken up the mountain.
The shepherds all have shelters of some sort on
the mountains and live up there with their sheep.
It could be some time before Evan Lewis returns
to Cwmddu, and that for the briefest of visits to
replenish his food supplies. I can show you how
to reach him, though the walk is a demanding
one, and it will take you most of a day to get there
and back."

"There is one thing which puzzled me,"
Holmes said. "I refer to the rumour which I overheard in the bar-room of the Black Lion that
Henry Harper had died of fright. I accept that it is
untrue, but whoever invented such a rumour
would surely also have had in mind what
frightened him."

So this was the question which Holmes really
wanted to ask, and who more likely to give an
honest answer than a parson!

"Ah!" Mr Ferris answered. "Perhaps it is a pity
that my son James is, as I told you, with his
mother at my sister's house in Clyro – but then
I doubt that he knows more than he told me.
According to James, it was common gossip
among the village children that the unfortunate
Mr Harper had obviously had an encounter with,

and I use his words, 'the fearsome spectral hound which haunts those woods'. 'They say', and I am still quoting, 'that on still, moonless nights, its terrible, mournful cries can be heard, even here in the village of Cwmddu'."

"And there is such a local legend?" I enquired. "I have recently read a book upon that very subject, though I don't recall reading of any spectral hounds."

"You anticipate me, Dr Watson. I too had not heard of such a creature, though I have several books in my library which touch upon the subject of local legend. I went so far as to enquire of some of my parishioners, usually most ready to regale me with tales of the supernatural. None of them knew of any kind of tradition of haunting in those woods. One must conclude that it is no more than children's fantasy, though it does have that ring to it of authentic legend. I'm sorry Mr Holmes that I cannot be more helpful."

....

It was mid-afternoon when we left the parsonage, time enough, Holmes decided, for a visit to the gate where Harper had met his death. It was a spot I had already heard described so many times, that it held no surprises when I did, at last, have sight of it. The gate was, perhaps, in an even greater state of dilapidation than I had expected. It had clearly not been used in many years. The gate hinges looked to be rusted solid, and I imagined that any attempt to release them by moving the gate, might well achieve no more than the final collapse of the woodwork of the gate itself!

I suppose that I had expected Holmes to make a careful examination of the spot. He did not, though for some reason he suddenly showed a cheerfulness that I had not seen for the last three days. He gave no reason for his sudden change of mood, and it was not until after dinner at the inn that he gave me any real clue as to his future intentions. That came in the suggestion that we should go early to our beds. Tomorrow, we were to visit Evan Lewis on the mountain. If the walk were as demanding as Mr Ferris had claimed, then by setting out early, we would largely avoid the added discomfort of climbing under a hot sun.

....

Even without the hot sun, the walk was indeed, "demanding". We had covered what must have been no more than half the distance before I had begun to feel some exhaustion, and was becoming increasing annoyed at Holmes' refusal to rest. We could have hired two horses, but Holmes would not travel on horseback, claiming that the last time he had done so he'd found it too painful to sit down for several days afterward. I told him that if he ate more, he would acquire sufficient fat over his nether parts to overcome that problem. His counter to that was that if I ate less, then I would not become so rapidly exhausted by what was little more than a brisk walk. I'm sure that the conversation would have become even more acrimonious, if only I'd had the breath to continue it!

I suppose that I should have felt some gratitude at finding Evan Lewis in the immediate vicinity of his somewhat makeshift hut, and not some still greater distance up the mountain with his sheep. I was not even convinced of the need for this visit. Anything Lewis might tell us had surely been described by Dr Price.

Unlike the two elderly ladies in Cwmddu, about whose reluctance to talk Mr Ferris had warned us, Lewis was obviously flattered that "two important gentleman from London" had climbed all that way just to talk to him.

All of Holmes' questions to Lewis were clearly directed at one thing. He wanted to know the exact position of Harper's body as it had lain on the ground. That could only be done by Lewis himself lying down on the grass to demonstrate. My cap was borrowed to substitute for the book which Harper had been holding. I still saw little point in the exercise. Price had said the body was lying on its back and that the lividity marks which had formed on the back showed quite clearly that it had not been moved from the position in which it had originally fallen. Holmes was taking an unconscionable time in what he was doing with Lewis's assistance, and I found my attention wandering to the several remarkable views which were visible from that height. "Breathtaking" seemed the apt description!

I was, therefore, quite startled by Holmes' sudden announcement that, "We're ready, Watson! Mr Lewis will attempt to hold that position, while you draw it. And don't tell me that you can't draw. I would imagine that your training in human anatomy should render the task a relatively simple one. And you see that I've brought in my bag more than some light refreshment – a sketch pad and pencils."

....

We returned to the Gospel Inn late that afternoon, and I must confess to having quite enjoyed the return journey – downhill! Holmes wanted to spend some time in his room before dinner, and took my sketch with him, though I had offered to do some tidying up on it. He had looked at it several times on our way down from the mountain, and each time I had seen it, I'd felt sure that I'd got something wrong in the drawing, something to do with the position of the limbs. All I can say is that it looked unnatural. But, since Holmes seemed more than satisfied, I did not press the point.

I went to my own room to do the same thing I imagined Holmes would be doing – to rest on my bed. I stirred myself from it in plenty of time to change my clothes for dinner and, having still some minutes to spare, went across the landing to Holmes' room to ensure that he had not gone to sleep.

He was neither asleep, nor was he properly

dressed. Having knocked on his door and been invited to enter, I found him apparently engaged in throwing himself about on the bed! On seeing me enter, he stepped down onto the floor, and as if I had just witnessed something entirely normal, he said, simply, "It's no use, Watson. I don't see how it can be done."

"You don't see how *what* can be done?"

"The book, of course. You said that your sketch of the body looked unnatural. It does, though the reason is not through any shortcomings in your artistry. And the most unnatural thing about it is the position of the hand holding the book. I asked Lewis several times if he was certain that's how it was. He *was* certain. The book is clenched in the right hand, the right arm stretched out and across the body. But the palm of the hand is turned outwards. I have tried falling in every conceivable way, and I cannot duplicate that palm outwards position."

"And this tells you something?" I enquired.

"Oh! Yes! Watson. It tells me that Mrs Harper is right. There is 'something not right about the whole business'. But then I knew that yesterday when I saw the gate."

"But you hardly looked at it – and it looked an ordinary enough gate to me."

"Perhaps if I said, 'gateway' rather than 'gate'."

"Then I'd say it's a perfectly ordinary gateway!"

"What amazes me, Watson, is the number of people who must now have looked at that gateway – and all reached the same conclusion as yourself. Yet it is a quite *extra*ordinary gateway. You see, Watson, it leads nowhere. There is no trace of there ever having been a road or path beyond it. Indeed, it apparently serves no purpose whatsoever. So why, I ask, is it there at all?"

I could see what Holmes was driving at, but I didn't see that it helped.

"That, my friend, is something we may better understand if you will undertake for me a simple, if possibly tedious, mission."

"Anything." I said.

"I want you to return to London. You've spoken of a friend of Stamford's, an artist, an illustrator whose work I recall your greatly admiring."

"Paget," I said. "Sydney Paget."

"Find Mr Paget and take him to see Mrs Harper. I want him to draw that watercolour which she says she's looked at for twenty years. Pay Mr Paget any reasonable fee he asks. I'm not interested in the man or the dog in the painting, just the gateway and the gate. And I want you back with it as quickly as possible."

"You're staying here?"

"Yes, Watson. I still have several things to do – like discovering whether that wood behind the gate *is* haunted, and if so, by what?"

Watson's sketch of Evan Lewis

Drawing of the gateway made from Mrs Harper's description

Chapter Five

The Howling Dog

I left Hay for London on the Saturday morning, returning late on the following Tuesday afternoon. I had telegraphed Holmes the time of my intended arrival and he met me at Hay Station.

"You have it?" was his first question.

I assumed that he referred to the drawing. "Yes," I told him, "though I'm not sure that it's quite what you expected."

"You mean, Watson, that according to Mrs Harper, her husband said 'the gate was wrong'. But now that you have seen both what Harper thought was the actual gate and the drawing you cannot see any very obvious difference."

"If you knew that already, why have I just been all the way to London, spent the whole of Sunday trying to find Sydney Paget, and then . . ."

"Steady, Watson! I didn't 'know' it. It was only on Sunday that I guessed it myself, but I still would have needed your help. I still needed to have that guess confirmed. And I'm also hoping that you've discovered the answer to something that continues to puzzle me."

I wasn't aware that I'd discovered the answer to anything, so I let Holmes finish.

"I imagine that Mr Paget most probably did his first rough sketch, certainly in the presence of Mrs Harper and, I assume, also yourself."

"Yes. He did."

"Then you must have seen, even at that point, that the sketch and the gate were, at least in their general appearance, the same."

"I did."

"Now recall our first interview with Mrs Harper. When she mentioned her husband's remark about the gate being 'wrong', she made no other comment upon it except that he'd never said what was wrong with it. Yet at the time she told us that, she already knew of the close resemblance between the actual gate and the one in her husband's painting."

I was pleased to tell Holmes that it was not a matter which had escaped me, even if, in truth, it was Mrs Harper who had raised it!

"She had simply assumed," I said, "that 'wrong' did not refer to its general appearance, but merely to some detail. She did say that her husband had an unusually sharp eye for detail."

"Perhaps so," was all that Holmes replied.

During the time of that conversation, we had

reached the outside of the station. Holmes had hired a trap, not dissimilar in appearance to that of Mr Ferris. Holmes was laughing!

"Have no fear Watson! I drove it here myself without great discomfort. The springing is quite good. With only two of us, and little luggage, I can at least promise you a less hazardous journey than the one you are obviously recalling."

In fairness to Holmes, the journey was a deal less unpleasant than I'd expected, though not sufficiently so that I dared concentrate my attention upon anything other than remaining in my seat. In consequence, my own desire to learn what Holmes had been doing in my absence, had to wait – much longer than expected!

I had unpacked, washed and changed for dinner and, at Holmes suggestion, joined him in his room with half an hour to spare before the evening meal. I found him seated on his bed and contemplating the washstand. He had removed the jug and basin and had propped the sketches side by side against the tiled splashback – mine of Evan Lewis, and Sydney Paget's of the gateway.

"What do you think, Watson?"

"That I'm a dreadful artist!" I replied.

"You probably are, Watson. But then, I'm sure that Mr Paget would make a dreadful doctor. It really is of no consequence. Put the two sketches together – and you have the solution to one part of this mystery. Why did the dying Henry Harper go back to what everyone assumes was the wrong gate, and how did he come to die there?"

How Holmes could see all that in two sketches, I had no idea. I suggested, I suppose sarcastically, that they had also told him why Harper had taken a book of poems with him.

"No, Watson. They don't, because he didn't!"

I had already sensed that Holmes was not, in fact, going to tell me anything – anything, that is, that made sense to me. For what small consolation it was, he did, for once, offer a reason.

"Indulge me, Watson. There is such a tale here yet to unfold. All of it, I do not yet know myself, but I ask you to give me the pleasure of savouring that unfolding for just a little longer."

"How much longer?" I asked.

"Who knows? The stage is set. Now we wait."

"For what?"

"Rain, Watson. Rain and darkness!"

....

It promised to be a dull evening, and was in every respect. Before we had finished our evening meal, it had, indeed, begun to rain, that kind of steady rain which, perhaps for no very logical reason, looks set to continue for some hours. Normally light at that time of year until about nine, the lamps in the inn had been lit by half past seven. With such a wet, black night outside, few appeared in the bar-room that evening, and none stayed for long. Having been asked not to question Holmes upon the one topic which most intrigued me, I found it difficult to sustain any kind of conversation. I did feel entitled to point out that we now had both "rain and darkness", but that I was still unaware of anything unusual having happened. The only reply that I got was, "It will, Watson, and you will be very aware of it when it does."

I went to my bed at eleven, and remember nothing until I was shaken out of a sound sleep by Holmes.

"I'm sorry, Watson. I had not thought there would be any need for my wakening you. I should perhaps have accounted for the tiring effects of your long train journey."

He gave me no time to answer before crossing to the window and pulling back the curtains. It was obviously still some time in the middle of the night. He had already lit the lamp by my bedside and I could see that he was fully dressed. I looked at my watch. It was two in the morning!

Not turning his gaze from the window, he said, "There's no need to dress, Watson. Put on a dressing gown and join me at the window."

Not yet fully awake, I dutifully did as I was bidden and joined Holmes. I was astonished at what I saw. There seemed to be no single house in the village in which there was not a lighted window. Though the rain was as steady as ever, I could see people – at windows, in doorways, some even standing in the rain, in the middle of the street!

"What's happened?" I asked.

"It was plainer before," Holmes answered. "Perhaps if we open the window."

There was a rush of wet, cold air. I stepped back. I could hear the hiss of the rain then, some-where, a voice, briefly raised, though I could not catch the words. But there was something else, like an eerie, mournful cry. It seemed distant, yet so ill-defined I could not be certain that it was a sound carried upon the wind or merely one created by the wind itself. I listened intently.

"It's a dog!" I declared. "It's a dog howling. It must be quite far off."

"Yes, Watson," Holmes answered. "It is the sound of a howling dog."

"But the lights, the people, Holmes. A howling dog doesn't bring a whole village out onto the street in the middle of the night, much less on a night as wet as this!"

Holmes closed the window, but left the curtains drawn back.

"Not in *any* village, Watson, yet clearly it does in this village. But that should not come as a total surprise to you. Remember breakfast at the Black Lion – and the reaction of the landlord when you innocently joked about the Gospel Inn having no 'howling dogs'. And then there was Mr Ferris's story – his child's description of the 'fearsome spectral hound' known, he said, to the village children, yet apparently unheard of by their elders."

"Really, Holmes! You're not seriously suggest-ing that what we've just heard is the cry of some phantom hound!"

"No, Watson. I *know* that it isn't. But that is a

piece of knowledge not shared by those down there in the street."

Holmes looked at his watch.

"I need to keep close observation on what is happening outside for at least the next hour. I imagine that nothing *will* happen until somewhere around dawn. I suggest, Watson, that you therefore return to your bed and get what sleep you can. I expect to wake you early, at which time we shall be setting off upon what I hope will prove to be a most rewarding piece of exploration."

"And am I allowed to ask, 'For what?'."

"You are, Watson, and I will tell you, though do not blame me if it serves only to prevent your having those few more hours of peaceful sleep which you so obviously need. In the morning, I hope to discover the whereabouts of Thomas Harper's house, perhaps even of Thomas Harper!"

....

Holmes came to my room again at a little after six. This time, he did not have to wake me. Just as he'd predicted, I had not had a restful night and, tired of tossing and turning had, some minutes before, given up any idea of sleep and got up. Holmes sat on my bed while I finished dressing. I asked if he knew exactly where we were going.

"'Exactly', no. Approximately, yes – but I expect no difficulty in finding the place. Four men left the village at dawn, more than an hour since. They are but recently returned. I had foreseen the small possibility that they might have left in the early hours of this morning, when we heard the dog, but I doubted that they would have stomach enough for that. I was right – which is fortunate. It will make retracing their steps very much easier."

I had, at least, guessed correctly that we would take the road that led to what I had now christ-ened "Harper's gate". Nor did I need Holmes' skills to see that four others had walked and re-turned that way, sometime earlier. The "road" was little better than a track with many patches of no more than bare earth. The rain must have ceased during the night, leaving the ground in a state which showed near perfect footprints.

Since the tracks clearly led farther on, I was surprised when Holmes stopped. Though we had not yet reached "Harper's gate", we had reached the stone wall that marked the boundary between the road and the wooded area beyond it. Holmes leaned over the wall and from somewhere, I sup-posed a well-chosen hiding-place in the under-growth, he pulled out a long, bulky object wrap-ped in oiled silk. Whatever it was, it was bound at each end with rope, then tied across in a manner which supplied it with a handle for carrying. He handed the bundle to me. It was heavy!

"I brought it here, Watson. It would therefore seem a fair division of labour for you to carry it the rest of the way. It may not be far."

"What is it?"

"Tools, Watson, should it prove necessary for us to do some excavation."

....

The tracks we were following led past the gate, apparently without pause, but stopped at a point some hundred yards beyond it. Here, the owners of the footprints, had obviously climbed over the wall and made their way into the woods which lay beyond. Holmes and I followed. I'm certain that I would quickly have lost all trace of the tracks in the dense undergrowth. I was therefore grateful that I had only to follow Holmes, who seemed able to move little more slowly through fern and briar than he had upon the road! Not far into the trees he stopped again.

"This is it, Watson," he said.

To me, it was just trees!

"Look above you, Watson. The trees in this area are shorter than those surrounding it. Look at the thickness of the trunks. They're younger. Fifty or more years ago, it was certainly a clearing."

"What now?" I asked.

"A systematic search. If we cross the area in a number of straight lines, we should find what we're looking for. Leave the tools for the moment. We're seeking evidence of the foundations of a house. There may be none actually visible – but the earth over those foundations will be shallower than the surrounding soil. And that will show itself on the surface in a number of possible ways. The vegetation may be of a different colour, or of a different kind, or more stunted in growth. Find that sort of variation which occurs in what looks like more or less straight lines and you've found what we're looking for. It may prove easy, it may be difficult. Let's hope it's the former. You start in that direction – towards that rowan."

Half an hour later Holmes called me over to where he was searching. He pointed to the ground.

"Wild orchids, Watson."

"Yes," I said. "I see that, and quite a lot of them."

"Don't look where they are, Watson. Look where they're not. I imagine they like moisture."

I could see what Holmes meant. There was a distinct strip of ground, on which there were none, though they grew plentifully on either side of it. I fetched the "tools" – which were two spades and a small pickaxe.

It took no more than a few minutes to uncover a line of roughly trimmed stones, traces of loose mortar, and a considerable quantity of charred timber, the charring having almost completely preserved it from any kind of rot.

"It's enough," Holmes said, resting on his spade. "I think we have found Thomas Harper's house. With sufficient time, I suspect that we might also find Thomas Harper, but there may be easier ways of establishing his presence."

"Holmes," I said, "I really don't understand how you could have deduced all of this, but let me ask you one question now. I know it has to do with the dog we heard, but why did anyone come here, and what did they expect to find?"

"I can tell you why they came here. They weren't looking for the house. They were looking for the dog's footprints. They should, of course, have known that there would be none. If the dog was flesh and blood, then it was unlikely that it was ever here. If it had indeed been spectral, then it would not have left any footprints. But we must be grateful that the villagers of Cwmddu are *not* capable of such logic. Otherwise, they would not have come, and we would not have found Thomas Harper's house!"

I didn't immediately answer him. Holmes probably concluded that he had simply added to my confusion. For once, he would have been wrong. I had recalled that we had not yet had breakfast!

"I am not being difficult, Watson. If I tell you that *I* was responsible for arranging last night's howling dog, then you are in a position to know everything that I do. Whatever happened to Thomas Harper and his house, it may have been a long time ago, but it was certainly dramatic. It was dramatic enough to find a whole village still silent upon the subject – a village that still fears the sound of a dog howling in the night. And we find a respectable country doctor who has not only lied but who has quite deliberately falsified evidence concerning a man's death. Serious offences, I'm sure you agree. And why did he do it? To protect that same secret of what happened in this place, perhaps fifty years ago. I ask you Watson, 'What strange manner of thing could it have been?'."

Chapter Six

Cwmddu's Secret

I saw the question Holmes had posed as just a subject for endless speculation, but he assured me that was not the case. He seemed certain that by the end of the day we would know the whole truth.

"And if, Watson, as I suspect, you are equally interested in the answer to another question – 'When might we hope to have some breakfast?', the answer is, 'Just as soon as we have covered up all traces of our visit here'."

The earth we had dug out was put back and the disturbed area covered with rotting plant material which lay about in profusion beneath the undergrowth. Back on the road, Holmes carefully obliterated those few footprints which would have shown that we had left it. We then walked on, away from the village, for another hundred yards, before turning back. Anyone without Holmes' skill in tracking, should they notice our footprints, would merely conclude that we had taken an innocent, early morning constitutional. The tools had been rewrapped and tied. These Holmes returned to their original hiding-place. Why all of this was really necessary, I did not know, but I was not anxious to set Holmes off upon any lengthy explanations which might still further delay our eating!

I should have expected that the events which had occurred during the night in Cwmddu would not be forgotten with the coming of the morning. To reach the inn, we had to walk the length of the village street. There we passed two groups of people who had clearly been engaging in earnest conversation. But on both occasions the conversation had ceased before we were properly within earshot, and did not resume until we had walked for some distance on.

Since our boots and even the bottoms of our trousers were considerably spattered with mud, I had assumed that on reaching the inn, we would first go to our rooms. Holmes had no such intention. Not only did we go straight to the dining-room, but it was almost as if he were anxious to draw attention to the state of our feet.

"I apologise," he said to the landlord. "Had we realised the state of our boots earlier, we would have gone to our rooms and changed. But you must blame it upon your bracing Welsh air. I must confess that both Dr Watson and I have returned from our constitutional with little else on our minds than the quite voracious appetites which the walk seems to have given us!"

"It was noticed that you were gone out very early," was the reply. "We was only concerned that it wasn't 'cause of you sleeping badly. We'd been thinking you might have heard the disturbance in the night."

I felt it best to let Holmes continue to do the talking.

"Dr Watson has already told me that he heard nothing. He is blessed with being a heavy sleeper. I did wake, myself, and hear some commotion in the street, but I fear that in the act of considering whether it merited my getting out of a warm and comfortable bed to see more, I must have fallen asleep again. I trust it was nothing of too serious a nature."

"No more," we were told, "than a mishap, though bad enough for those it happened to at the time. It was the Watkins' house. Old, you see, and not in very good repair, like most in this village. Last night's wind and rain brought down a dozen slates off the roof. Near flooded out inside, they were, and they with five children, and one not out of its cradle. It was where to sleep them and to try and save their furniture from the damage, you see. Walking past this morning, as like you'd not even have noticed nothing," he added, "it being the roof at the back of the house."

There was not very much opportunity for private conversation over breakfast, though

Holmes did remark that he was now beginning to understand how a whole village could have succeeded in keeping secret what he was certain had been some very remarkable event – and keeping that secret for so many years.

"You could say that it's only because they are such accomplished liars. It's more than that, Watson. Living in a city, it's easy to forget just how close these isolated rural communities can become – secretive, intensely loyal, overly protective, even to a point where they will break the law, and go on breaking it to protect their own. You don't understand, Watson, but you will. We've just had one interesting demonstration of the kind of thing I'm saying. The story of the roof and the displaced family is clearly total invention, yet I am certain that were you to ask anyone in this village they would confirm every detail of it. It would not surprise me to find ladders at the back of the Watkins' house, for the apparent purpose of repairing a roof which was never damaged."

I finished breakfast with only one thing clear in my mind. Holmes was absolutely right when he said that I did not understand. I did take some consolation in the fact that he had repeated his assurance that I would, "before the day was out". I found less consolation in his announcement on how we would occupy ourselves until that time!

We would first go to our rooms and remove our muddy clothes. Holmes had then to compose a letter which we were to deliver personally to the house of Dr Price in Hay. We were to spend the day in Hay, not returning to Cwmddu until early evening. This, Holmes told me, was for the same reason that we had taken some pains to conceal the fact of our discovery early that morning. Not only must we appear not to be in possession of that knowledge, but we must afford ample opportunity for anyone wishing to check that we were not. And if all that took me no nearer to understanding what Holmes was about, nor did it lessen my one real concern – the prospect of a double journey in that vehicle which, on these roads, might have been more appropriately named a "death-trap"!

....

We did at least reach Hay without serious mishap. The letter to Price was delivered, at a time which I supposed to have been deliberately chosen, when the Doctor was already out upon his morning rounds. Holmes was quite delighted to discover that we had arrived in Hay on the occasion of a book auction. It was there that we spent most of the day. I found it boring. Holmes appeared to enjoy it, though all that he bought was two books, one a collection of engravings by Thomas Bewick, the other an obscure Latin thesis by a man called Purkenje, read before the University of Breslau in 1823 – upon the subject of finger impressions!

We returned to Cwmddu about mid-evening, in time, I assumed, for dinner at the inn. But we did not go into the village. We turned off just before it onto the road we had followed that morning, the road which led to "Harper's gate". We had to abandon the trap after the first half mile, and walk the rest of the way to the gate. Naturally, I enquired as to the purpose of this second visit in the day.

"We have an assignation, Watson, one which I trust you will find to be both instructive and informative."

He had barely spoken the words before we heard footsteps on the road and, a moment later, observed the approaching figure of Dr Hywel Price. The manner of his walk was sufficient to suggest that he was not in good temper, a deduction amply confirmed by his opening remark!

"I trust, Mr Holmes, that you are not about to waste my time. The hour is most inconvenient. Your note described the need for my presence here as 'imperative'. I'm here, though I remain at a complete loss to know for what precise purpose."

"You choose your words carefully," Holmes replied. "'Precise purpose'? No, I could not expect you to know that. So let me tell you what *I* already know. It may still not reveal my 'precise' purpose in arranging this meeting, but I'm sure that it will stimulate your powers of imagination.

"Fifty or more years ago, in a spot not very far from where we are standing, a man called Thomas Harper was murdered. His house was then burned to the ground – or the burning may itself have provided the means of his murder.

Such crimes are, regrettably, commonplace. That a group of people conspired to hide that crime is, again, not unusual. What I do find surprising is that that conspiracy of silence and deceit still goes on, half a century later. Still more surprising is that, apparently to protect that same ancient secret, a respectable medical practitioner is prepared to falsify evidence and perjure himself at a public inquest. These are criminal acts. Either offence, if discovered, would certainly result in his being struck from the medical register."

Nothing that Holmes had just said could really have surprised me. Most of it, he'd said before, except to go so far as stating that Thomas Harper had been murdered, though that possibility must surely have crossed my own mind. So, my thoughts at that moment, were not upon Holmes. I was trying rather to put myself into the place of Hywel Price and wondering how I would react in such a situation, assuming Holmes to have spoken the truth, and that I knew it! If that *were* the situation, then Price was showing a quite remarkable degree of self-control when he answered.

"I have to take you seriously, Mr Holmes. I would not judge you as a man to make such statements lightly. Yet, in some ways, you disappoint me. First, you appear to suggest that I am accessory to some crime which, if it ever took place, did so at a time when I was but an infant. Then you accuse me of professional misconduct, yet you offer nothing to support that accusation. It is, I suspect, because you have nothing. I ask myself, 'Why this meeting?' You clearly believe what you say, but if you can prove it, it is surely your duty to make your accusations to the police, not to me."

"Then let me tell you," Holmes replied, "exactly what happened on the night of Henry Harper's death. You came to the Gospel Inn, as you said, to see how Harper was responding to the drug which you had prescribed. You found that he had gone out. It was a reasonable assumption that he might have come here, and I believe that you followed him here only out of proper concern for the man's life. What you could not have anticipated was what you discovered upon your arrival.

"You found Henry Harper dead, but it was not at eight the next morning, nor was the body lying on the ground. Despite all the evidence to the contrary, Harper had remained convinced that the gate which he had found *was* the gate that had once led to his uncle's house. But why would he knowingly risk his life to visit the place yet again? Because, Dr Price, he now knew that he could prove himself right! He'd sensed that there was something wrong with the gate but, perhaps surprisingly, had not before realised what it was. It *was* the same gate but, since the last time he'd seen it, it had been rehung – upside down! And that had triggered one other memory. On what had been the top of the gate, was carved the name, Thomas Harper. Henry Harper killed himself, Dr Price, in trying to lift the gate from its hinges, and that is the position in which you found his body."

Holmes had moved over to the gate, near to the end at which it was hinged. He now bent down, flexing his knees, resting his left forearm on top of the gate and placing his right hand under one of the cross bars. It brought his right arm across his body, and the palm of his hand facing outwards. It was exactly as in my sketch of Harper's body, but turned upside down! The attitude of the body, which I had found so curious, now looked completely natural. Price remained silent.

"Perhaps you didn't know, but you must have guessed," Holmes continued, "why Harper had been trying to lift the gate when he died. If you could guess it, so might others. You couldn't allow his body to be found in that position. Rigor had set in but, with what I imagine was some difficulty, you removed it, laying it on the ground in as natural a position as was possible in the circumstances. You had found Harper within minutes of his death. Rigor had set in instantly but his blood had not yet congealed. Moving the body so soon after death, the blood would still resettle to the lowest position. The marks of lividity, formed when the blood congeals would betray nothing of what you'd done. But you still had one problem. The hand which had clutched the bar of the gate was fixed in that position, still obviously clutching, but now at nothing!

"That is why you placed the book in the hand. I don't know where you got it. It had to fit tightly. You must have at least had to return to Cwmddu for it. Having done that, you could leave the body to be rediscovered, as indeed it was next morning by Evan Lewis, the shepherd."

Price was clearly about to speak.

"Let me finish, Dr Price. You suggested that if I had any evidence of what I'd said, I should take it to the police. I have, and I could. The gate could be lifted to reveal the name of Thomas Harper. Of course, this gateway does not lead to what remains of Harper's house. That stands a hundred yards away from here, where it always was. It is difficult to obliterate all traces of a house. It is relatively easy to move a gateway. And I suspect that a little diligent digging would uncover some, if not all of the charred remains of Thomas Harper himself.

"You asked me, 'Why this meeting?' At its simplest, Dr Price, you can call it curiosity. I ask myself why a respectable medical practitioner would risk both his reputation and his professional status to protect a fifty year old secret. You paid me the compliment of accepting that I did not make my accusations lightly. Let me return that compliment by saying that I am equally certain that you would not have done what you did without a very good reason. I have not gone to the police, because I would first wish to know that reason. Convince me that the reason was good enough and I may still be prepared to forget what I know and everything that has just passed between us."

Though it might have appeared so, Holmes had offered Price no real choice. The Doctor's only hope of protecting the secret for which he had already risked so much was to do exactly as Holmes had asked. I am sure Holmes never doubted he could put Price into precisely that position – of having no alternative but to tell the whole story. What I cannot believe is that even Holmes could have expected a tale quite so frightening as the one which we were to hear later that same evening.

....

Thomas Harper arrived in the area of Hay, in 1814. He found and purchased a near derelict cottage about a mile from Cwmddu. Being a carpenter of some skill, he completely rebuilt and extended the house, finally replacing the rotted gateway which led to it from the road. He was a man wishing only to be left in peace and solitude. It was a wish respected by his "neighbours" and, for six years, Thomas Harper lived in that house, troubling none and none troubling him. And then, in 1821, the local shepherds, who had taken their flocks up the hills for the summer, began to lose sheep. Twelve were killed in a single night, each animal with its throat torn out, some part eaten. Extra men, armed with guns, kept a nightly watch, but the killings went on. The culprit was never once seen, not even glimpsed, but it was generally believed that the killer must be a wild dog and, from the terrible nature of the wounds it left, a beast of exceptional size and power.

Suddenly it was rumoured that Thomas Harper owned just such a dog. He was visited by men from the village of Cwmddu. The truth of the rumour was plain to see. Harper did indeed own such a dog, a monstrous black hound of terrifying appearance. There was an instant demand from the visitors that the dog be immediately destroyed, but Harper would have none of it. He said that he had found the dog, or the dog had found him. It had been with him since the winter. Against all appearances, he claimed it to be a gentle animal, and one that had become a good friend. It would take more than mere supposition for him to be persuaded to destroy it. And anyone else who might think to try could be certain of having good cause to regret it!

The visitors left. The sheep killing continued. Over the next weeks, the tension between Harper and his neighbours steadily grew. And it was in the midst of that situation that ten year old Henry Harper chose to visit his uncle.

We could now understand Thomas Harper's strange behaviour towards his nephew. We could still not have foreseen what was so quickly to follow.

"It was late August," Price said, "in the early evening of a dark, bleak day, with a wet mist rolling down from the hills. The Williams had a house in Cwmddu with some land at the back of it where they kept hens and a few livestock. Gladys Williams was working in the kitchen with two of her three children shouting and squealing around in some noisy game, so that it was not until she stopped to tell them to play more quietly that she realised that Mary, her four year old, was missing. Mary was not to be found in the house. By now it was turning quite dark. Lighting a lantern, Gladys Williams went out into the yard. Within a hundred yards of the house, she found her child – dead. The small body was horribly gored and drenched in blood. Standing above it was Harper's dog, itself covered in blood. On seeing Mrs Williams, it had run off, quickly vanishing into the mist."

Within the hour, every man, and some of the women of Cwmddu were marching upon Harper's house. All carried torches or lanterns. Several carried guns, or some other weapon. Harper had seen or heard their approach. Already, he had barricaded himself in the house and threatened to shoot the first who tried to enter it. The anger of the crowd was great, but still there remained some element of sanity. They wanted only the dog. The reply they got was that they could have it, but that they'd have to take both the dog and Harper himself, if they could!

"I do not know every detail, Mr Holmes. The crowd moved towards the house several times, only to retreat again when they were met with buckshot from the inside. But blind anger knows no limit. The final confrontation had to come, and it did when someone hurled a lighted torch through the window. The room was quickly in flames, and the fire had soon begun to spread through the rest of the timber building. There were two more shots from the house, then nothing. The crowd was suddenly silent.

"That silence was broken by near demented cries, not from the house, but from someone running from the direction of the village. It was one of the women who had remained behind. Desperately, she gasped out her story. The child had not been killed by the dog! Someone had left open the gate to a sty where a sow was lying with litter. The child had wandered into the sty. It was the sow who had savaged and killed it. Both sow and sty were covered in the child's blood. It was clearly the dog who had attempted to rescue the child, pulling it from the sty and driving off the sow. The blood on the dog was its own. What Mrs Williams had seen was the dog, still guarding the body of the child whose life it had vainly attempted to save."

Several attempts were made to get into the house to rescue its occupants, though all that now remained of it was a blazing inferno.

"What then happened Mr Holmes, you must see as the actions of a simple, deeply religious and God-fearing community, a community suddenly restored to sanity – and with it, the awful knowledge that they had just murdered an innocent man, because his dog had bravely tried to save the life of one of their children!"

There had been no sleep in Cwmddu that night. They could not confess their terrible crime. They were all murderers. If the law were to take its just and proper course, what would become of their families?

"The next day, some of the men had gone back to the still smouldering remains of the house. Harper had been a solitary man, perhaps with neither kith nor kin. They had not seen the young Henry and believed Harper had had no visitors. If they were to remove all visible traces of the house, perhaps none would miss it. They covered the foundations with earth and hoped that nature would quickly do the rest. But there was still the gateway. The curious passer by might seek to find where it led. So, they moved it a hundred yards, filling up the old gap with stones from the new. Even I, Mr Holmes, was not previously aware that they had rehung the gate, upside down!

"I said that the people of Cwmddu were God-fearing. For them, it was not over. They felt bound to silence, yet equally committed to finding some means of showing due penitence for their grievous sin. It was as if that wish were to be granted by God Himself!"

Ten days had passed since the death of Thomas Harper, ten days in which the first horror had begun to fade. It was in the early hours of the morning of the eleventh day that Cwmddu was awaked in the dark hours, wakened by the terrible mournful howling of a dog. It lasted a full hour. It came again the next night, and the next. Men set off from the village with guns, but found nothing. For four nights, there was silence – but then it began again.

"And so, Mr Holmes, Dr Watson, it went on, following no pattern, other than it was always upon moonless nights. It went on for seven years! And in that time no sheep were killed, and no dog, nor even a pawprint, was ever seen – though many hunted for it. Think what you will, gentlemen, but those who heard that howling, and that includes myself, still find it difficult to believe that they were the cries of a beast of flesh and blood and not some terrible and supernatural visitation sent by a vengeful God."

Holmes sat silent for some moments. "I've seen the fear and know that the legend lives on – but it was a long time ago . . ."

Price interrupted. "You asked about William Price in Hay. He is my uncle. He is the man who threw the burning torch through Harper's window. He still thinks of himself a murderer. Gladys Williams in Cwmddu is the woman who thought that the dog had killed her child. Emily Parry is the woman who ran, crying out through the night, desperate to tell her true story, but too late to stop a man's murder."

Chapter Seven

For Peace of Mind

Holmes and I returned to London on the following day. In contrast to the near silence of that first journey to Hay, Holmes was in a talkative mood.

It seems almost unnecessary to state that Dr Hywel Price had been given the undertaking that Cwmddu could keep its secret. No-one with any soul could have listened to such a story and decided otherwise.

I knew, therefore, that this was not a case which I could publish, at least not for some long time. Price himself had asked only that the secret remain so until none were left alive who had been there on that dreadful night, and that he had himself retired from medical practice. It was important, therefore, that my notes, in the event that I did want to use them at some future time, should be as complete as possible.

Other than the telling of the story, which I have

already recorded, there had on that same occasion, been an exchange of information between Holmes and Price which had done much to fill in the many gaps in my own knowledge.

Holmes had already hinted that the unexpected return of what I must call the "howling dog" was his own doing, and that its sole purpose was to lead us to the true whereabouts of the remains of Thomas Harper's house. His first brief sight of the gateway had told Holmes that there was something quite unusual about it. As he'd said, it led nowhere and appeared to serve no purpose. If Henry Harper was right about the gateway, then what had happened to the house? There was only one logical answer – "Nothing!" But what better way of making an object vanish than by moving the thing which most obviously fixes its position? It was a theory strengthened by a further examination of the gateway which Holmes had carried out during my absence in London. Certain details of its construction, like the finish of the ends of the upright timbers and their distance beyond the cross members, and signs that the fastening had been moved, convinced him that it was upside down. If the gate had been moved, it could not have been moved far without defeating the very purpose of moving it. The house must therefore be near, but what remained of it could be completely buried and almost impossible to find.

Holmes had been struck by Mr Ferris's curious story of the spectral hound, and the surprising reaction to my innocent joke with the landlord of the Black Lion. The thought of a connection with Harper's dog was irresistible. If it were true, then the reappearance of such a creature would surely arouse some curiosity – enough, Holmes wondered, for someone who knew the whereabouts of the missing house, to lead us to it? What Holmes had been less sure of was just how the deception might be arranged. I had guessed that the dog was the same animal I had heard on our first night at the Black Lion. But, if the landlord did know the secret of Cwmddu, then it might be difficult to persuade him to be party to any such scheme. That problem did not arise. The dog was, in fact the property of the potman, who lived a mile from Hay, in the direction of Cwmddu. He travelled to and from the inn on horseback, the dog running alongside. If it was wet, he apparently contrived to carry the animal, wrapped in a blanket, with him on the horse.

If the potman knew anything of the story, it had not prevented his willing co-operation, for a sufficiently attractive financial inducement! His instruction was merely to wait for a wet night, bring the dog to within a quarter mile of Cwmddu and tether it in the rain for fifteen minutes. As we heard, the dog had not failed loudly to express his habitual objection to getting wet!

I, in fact, had only one question of any importance upon a matter which still puzzled me. How did Holmes know that the name "Thomas

Harper" was carved on the bottom of the gate?

"I didn't, Watson, and I'm sure it isn't. It was logical to assume that something had once been there, something which Henry Harper had remembered and had hoped to find. A name was as good a guess as any and would have provided one possible reason for the gate having been rehung upside down. Because I intended to tell Price that it *was* there I had to keep what knowledge we already had secret until that moment. I needed the element of surprise. If Price had looked carefully, he'd have seen what I'd already seen. The bottom of the gate, having rested so long on the ground, was completely rotted. Nothing that could have been carved on it was likely to have survived. But I didn't give Price time to think. I couldn't. He might have realised that he was right when he suggested I could prove nothing I'd said about his moving the body, not, that is, beyond all shadow of doubt. He might even have realized that if the remains of Thomas Harper do lie under the house, who is to say that it *is* Thomas Harper!"

....

The day following our return to Baker Street, Holmes went alone to see Mrs Harper at Brown's Hotel. Obviously, I did ask what he'd told her, but Holmes would say no more than she seemed satisfied with what small assurances he'd been able to give her.

I did, several times in the next few days, look over the notes that I had made on the case. They did appear to be complete, yet always they left me with the feeling that something was missing. I might have pursued it with Holmes but that those same days brought another distraction – what promised to be a new case in which I might be able to assist Holmes in his investigation.

So, my thoughts about Cwmddu and "The Case of the Howling Dog", were put to the back of my mind, and might have stayed there, but for the arrival of an envelope, delivered by hand. It contained a brief note from Mrs Harper saying, first, that at the time Holmes received the note, she would already be on her way back to America. More surprising was the statement that she trusted that the enclosed fee was adequate recompense for Holmes' services. It was an unexpectedly large sum of money.

"You look surprised, Watson," Holmes said. "Perhaps you'd have been less so if I'd answered the question for which you were searching in your mind even as we returned on the train from Hay. It's about the book."

Of course, I knew that the book was important. That there was something wrong about the book in Harper's hand when his body was found must have been the clue that led Holmes to make the rest of his deductions.

"But Price did mention it," I said. "He explained that he *was* telling the truth when he said that he had the book in his carriage. It had almost fitted Harper's hand, but he'd had to remove some pages to make it fit. He'd assumed it was those missing pages that had first aroused your suspicions. And you agreed with him."

"No, Watson. I didn't agree. I merely did not disagree, and I had a reason. You remember our first meeting with Mrs Harper. I said there was something she had not told us, yet I was sure that, unwittingly, she had. I had some difficulty in working out what it was. There were several odd things – Harper's apparent reluctance to write letters, the fact that his wife had written a note for him to carry on his person, so that she might be found if he were to become ill, the absence of any writing materials among his possessions, the fact that he carried large sums of money and always paid in cash. It all pointed to one thing."

"That the man was illiterate!" I exclaimed.

"Yes, Watson, yet that possibility did not fit with a man who had the necessary skills and intelligence to have become so highly successful in business. And then you came to my rescue."

"I!"

"You brought to Baker Street a number of medical books. I have not read them all, though you know I am given to 'dipping' into them. It was as we were travelling to Hay on that first occasion, that something flashed into my mind, a condition of which I had read in one of your books, a condition called 'word blindness'."

I had not heard of it.

"It is not a defect of the vision, but rather of the

brain, an inability to remember or recognise the written word though the sufferer may be normal, even highly intelligent, in every other respect. I have looked it up since we returned home. You will find it in Ziemssen's *Cyclopedia of the Practice of Medicine*. The condition was first described by Kussmaul in 1878.

"I imagine that Henry Harper could write his name, perhaps even recognise a few words, but he could not read. I knew this the night we first visited Price. So, when he told us that Harper had complained of having nothing to read, I knew he was lying. I did not deny his suggestion that I had seen the book and become suspicious of its missing pages. Remember, Watson, I had never seen the book. Price had retrieved it from the Gospel Inn before we arrived. But it was enough that I knew Price was lying, enough to suppose that he had put the book into Harper's hand. I didn't then know when or why. It was my further examination of the gate, and then your drawing, that made me realize what Harper had been doing when he died. Your mission to London to obtain the drawing of the gate was merely to confirm what I had already supposed – that the gate *would* look the same as that in the painting, because it had been rehung upside down. From that discovery my other deductions all followed."

I still didn't see the reason for the large fee.

"For reasons you know, Watson, I could tell Mrs Harper very little, but I *could* explain the one thing which, from the beginning, was all that she had wanted to know – why her husband was carrying a book which she knew he couldn't read! I merely told her that the book was forced upon him in circumstances where he found himself unable to refuse it. My intention was not to deceive her. She is too intelligent a woman for that. She knew that I knew her husband's secret – his inability to read and write. Clearly it was something of which Henry Harper had felt deeply ashamed all of his life. Loyalty to her husband's memory would not allow his wife to reveal that secret after his death, even what she described as 'something not right about the whole business', was a conviction based solely upon that inability.

"You still wonder why the fee is so generous. It is payment for two things – the assurance that her husband's death was in no way unnatural, and the knowledge that I too will respect Henry Harper's secret, as I did in my conversation with Price. You might call this a fee for 'peace of mind'. There are, perhaps, times in all of our lives, when we too would pay dearly to have it!"

....

The last of the original villagers of Cwmddu died in 1888. Mrs Henry Harper died in 1894 and Dr Hywel Price in 1900. In the first two decades of this century, for a number of different and unrelated reasons, the houses in Cwmddu one by one became empty and the village was eventually deserted. Its name no longer appears upon the map. Only the ruins of its church still stand.